quotable impressions

printmaking with inspired citations

dawn daisley

quotable impressions
printmaking with inspired citations

Published by
Dawn Daisley Designs
www.dawndaisleydesigns.com

Copyright ©2018
Dawn Daisley
4249 Oak Beach
Oak Beach, NY 11702

Editorial Consultant, Margaret Daisley
Blue Horizon Books, www.bluehorizonbooks.com

Cover: Dawn Daisley; Ferns AV3

Print Impressions & Book Design:
Dawn Daisley, www.dawndaisleydesigns.com
dawndaisley.weebly.com

Publisher's Cataloging-in-Publication data:
Daisley, Dawn
quotable impressions
printmaking with inspired citations
ISBN 9780578424064

dedication

Thank you to all who have crossed my path.

This small book combines quotes (words) with printmaking (visuals) to create impressions which have inspired each other.

I love quotes. They stimulate, excite, motivate. Words that are well-crafted leave lasting impressions. They touch an emotional pulse point in our soul. Quotes add clarity of thought when one can't find expression. A quote can help to see light when all seems dark and gives an extra burst of hope and courage to persevere.

I love printmaking. It is a multi-process endeavour. Printmaking is a journey to create a visual impression on paper. It begins with the spark of inspiration to transfer to a print plate, inking with thoughtful palette, combining plate and paper on a printing press, and finally the excitement and surprise when pulling the print. I aspire to create magical moments or places where one can find respite within their imagination based on natural habitats.

I work with various techniques and mediums of printmaking. Some include traditional etching, sugar lift, soft-ground on zinc plates, collagraph prints that sometimes are expanded with oil and encaustic. The print impressions in this book are created with a non-toxic method of·hand-drawn open-bite polymer solar plates and are etched in the sun.

I became aware of transitory stations along life's path when observing distinctive natural elements surround me. Metamorphosis, season changes, ocean tides, and shifting sands inspire over and over as these discoveries re-shape with beauty and dignity. I believe it is a lifelong task to know who we are and how we fit into this world.

The influence of dominant discourse within our culture can sometimes inhibit individuality and make self-expression difficult. Visual and literary arts are always being defined and re-defined with the development of new avenues for expression. It is my desire to combine and merge new artistic expression with technology and traditional artistic methods to build new art forms from previously forged foundations.

Please enjoy.
Dawn

try to forget what objects
you have before you — a
tree, a house, a field, or
whatever. Merely think, 'here is
a little square of blue, here an
oblong of pink,
here a streak of yellow,' and paint
it just as it looks to you, the
exact colour and shape, until it
gives you your own impression
of the scene before you.

— Claude Monet
painter

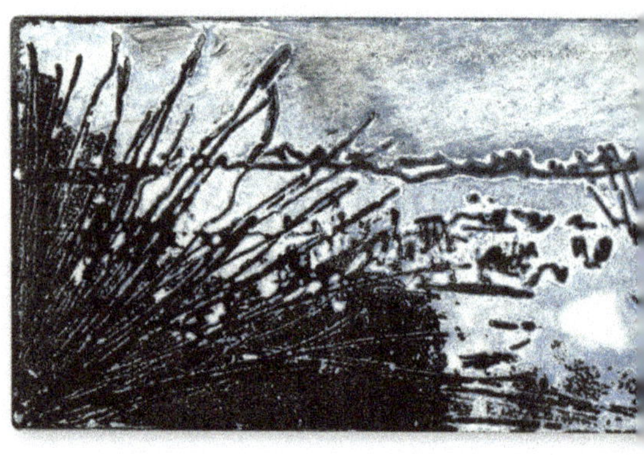

my soul is full of longing
for the secret of the sea,

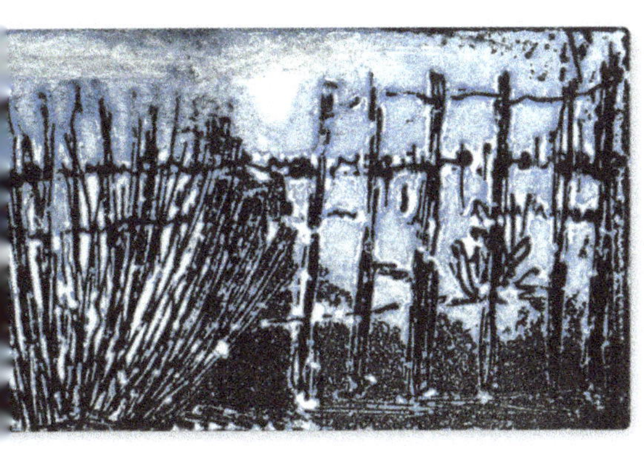

and the heart of the great

ocean sends a thrilling

pulse through me.

— *Henry Wadsworth Longfellow*
poet & educator

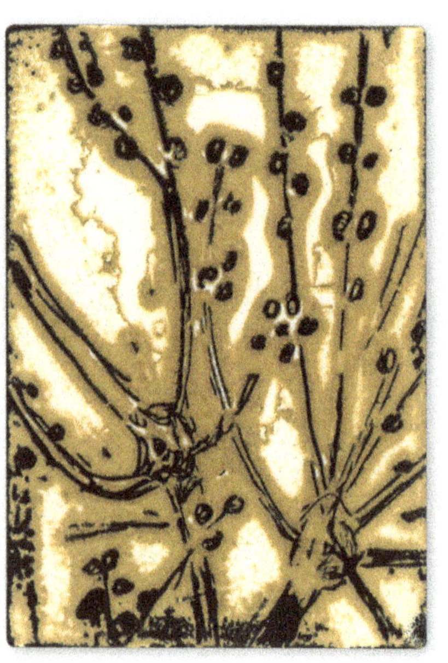

i shall become a master in this art only after a great deal of practice.

— *Erich Fromm*
philosopher

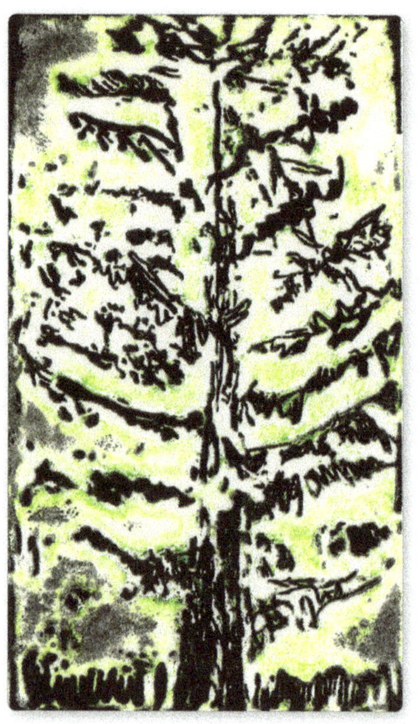

an intense anticipation itself transforms possibility into reality; our desires being often but precursors of the things which we are capable of performing.

— *Samuel Smiles*
author

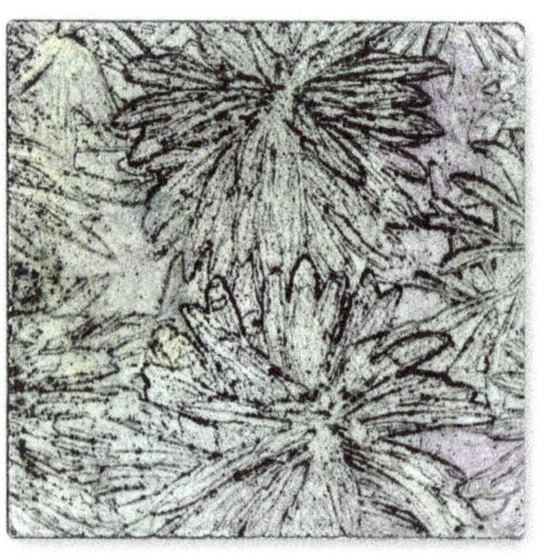

r eminding one another of
the dream that each of us
aspires to may be enough for
us to set each other free.

— Antoinne de Saint-Exupery
writer & aviator

hope is the thing with
feathers that perches
in the soul — and sings the
tunes without the words —
and never stops at all.

— *Emily Dickinson*
writer, poet

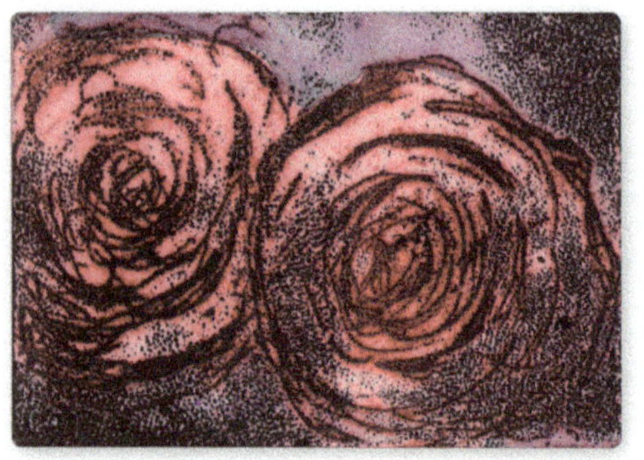

but he who dares not
grasp the thorn should
never crave the rose.

— Anne Brontë
novelist & poet

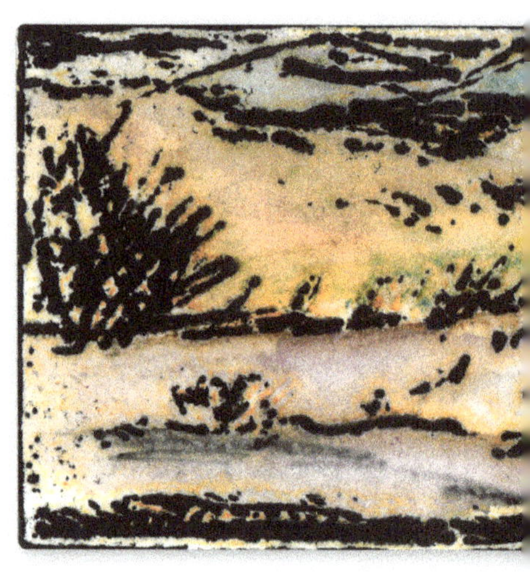

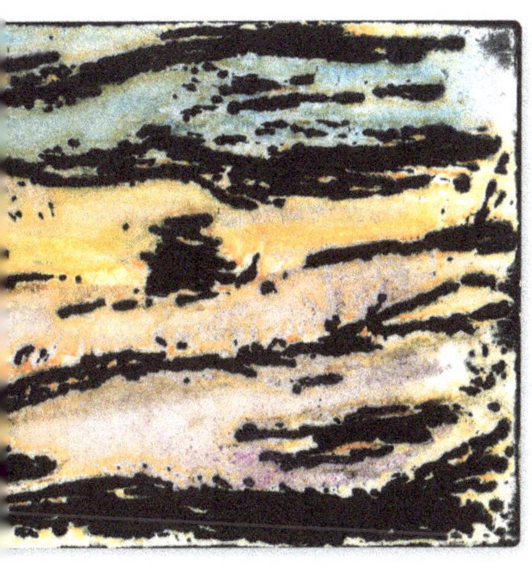

your head is a living
forest full of songbirds

— e.e. cummings
poet, painter, essayist,
author & playwright

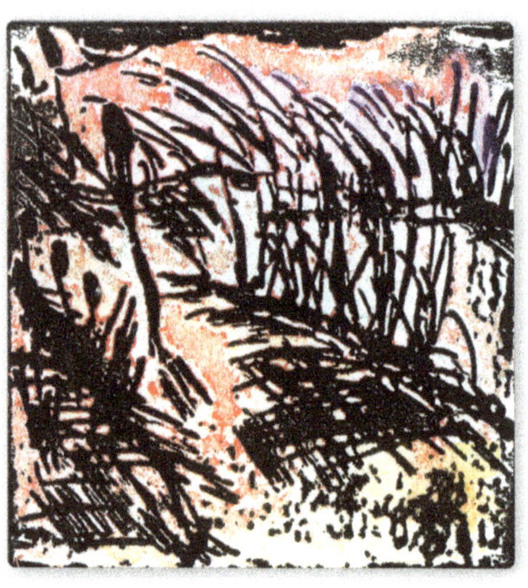

Live in the sunshine, swim the sea, drink the wild air.

— Ralph Waldo Emerson
philosopher, essayist & poet

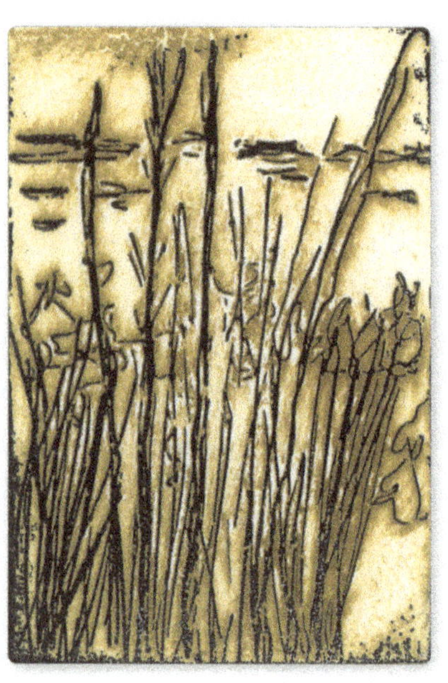

each of the beings
necessary to our existence
whose disappearance takes
away with him a whole world
of feelings that no other
relationship can relive.

— *Eugène Delacroix*
painter

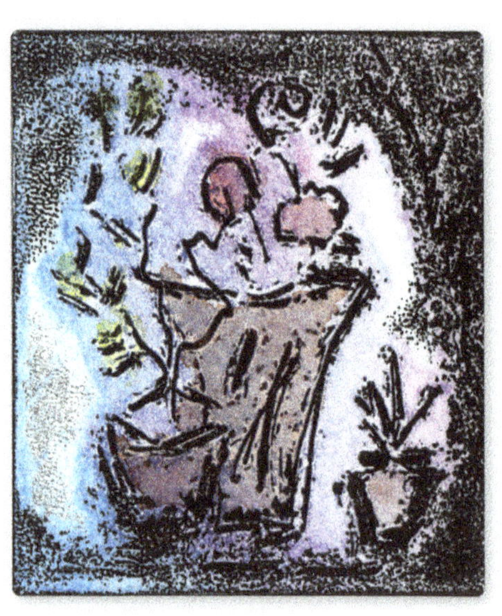

the things that we love
tell us what we are.

— *Thomas Aquinas*
theologian & scholastic philosopher

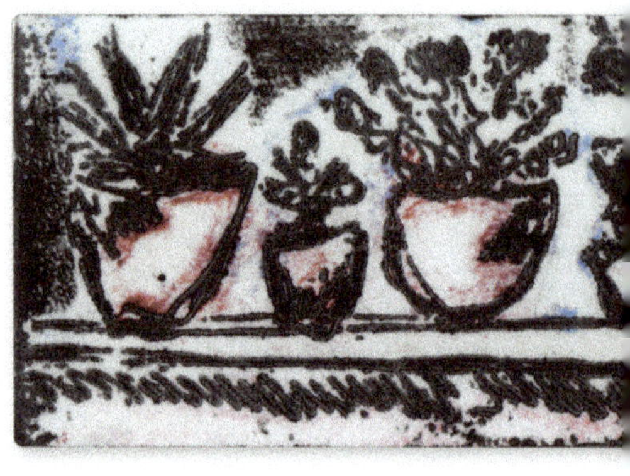

we cannot conceive of any end or limit to the world,

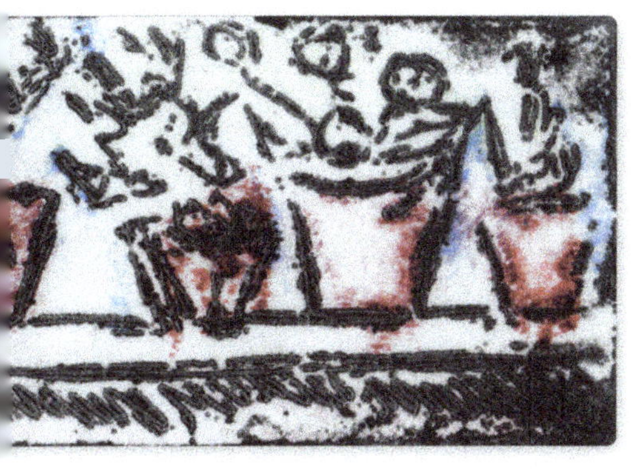

but always as of necessity

it occurs to us that there is

something beyond.

— *Francis Bacon*
philosopher, statesman,
scientist, jurist & author

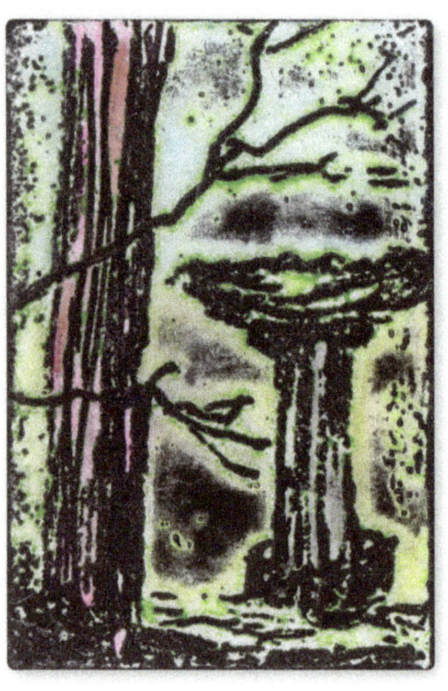

Something resides in
this heart that is not
perishable, and life is more
than a dream.

— Mary Wollstonecraft
writer, philosopher &
advocate of women's rights

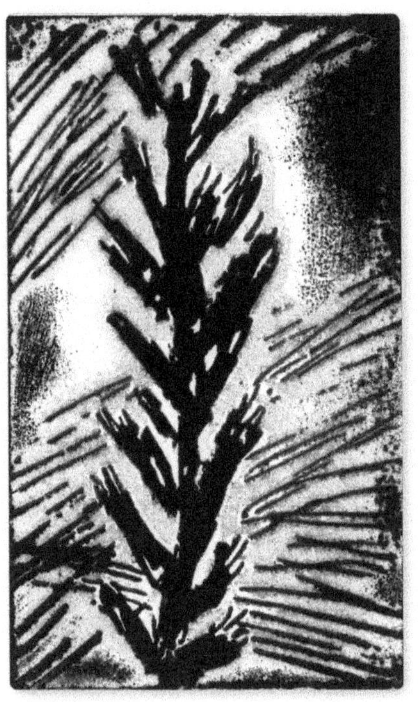

When an inner situation
is not made conscious,
it appears outside as fate.

— Carl Gustav Jung
psychiatrist & psychotherapist,
founder of analytical psychology

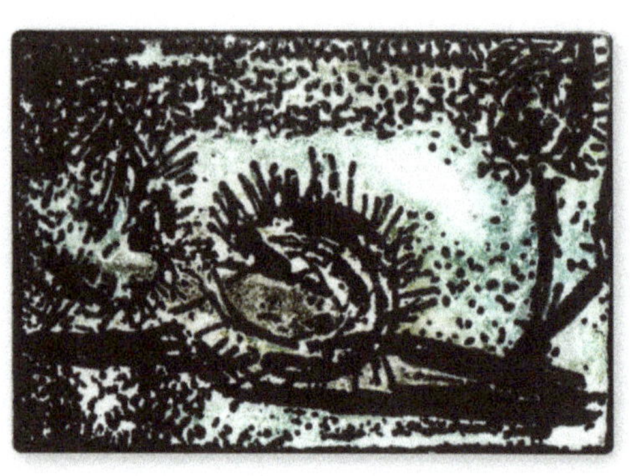

truth, like gold, is to be
obtained not by its growth,
but by washing away from it
all that is not gold.

— *Count Lev Nikolayevich Tolstoy*
author

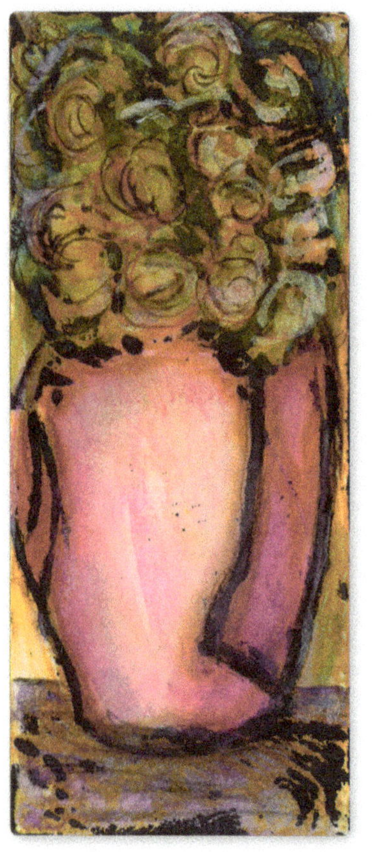

by means of an image we are often able to hold on to our lost belongings. But it is the desperateness of losing which picks the flowers of memory, binds the bouquet.

— *Sidonie Gabrielle Colette*
mime, actress, journalist & novelist

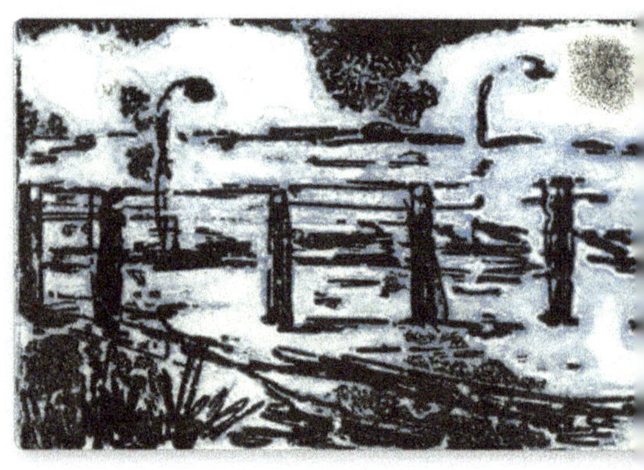

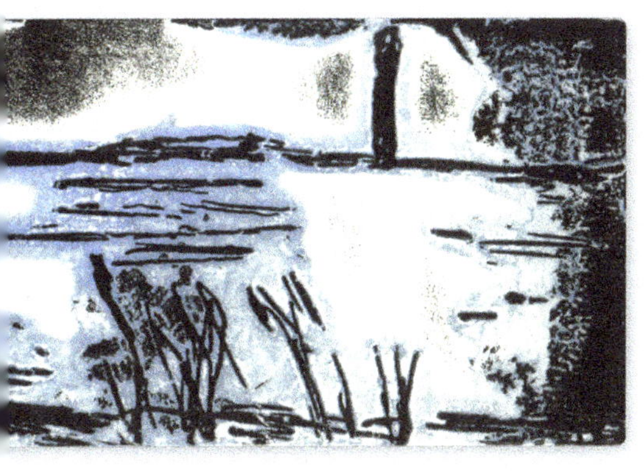

the universe will reward for taking risks on its behalf.

— Shakti Gawain
personal development author

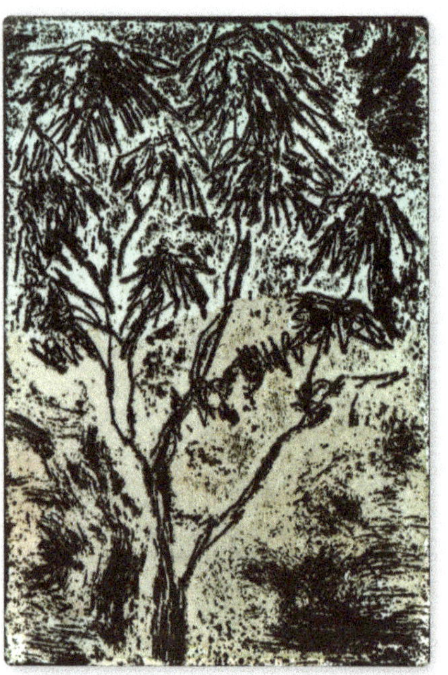

Change is the handmaiden nature requires to do her miracles with.

— *Samuel Langhorne Clemens*
writer, humorist, publisher & lecturer

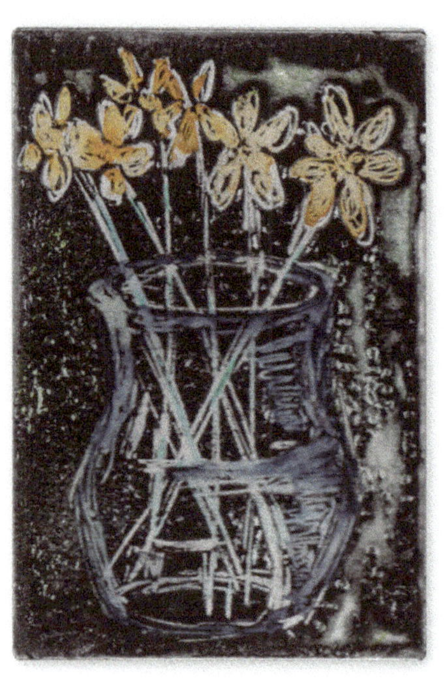

nothing can cure the soul
but the senses, just as
nothing can cure the senses but
the soul.

— *Oscar Wilde*
poet & playwright

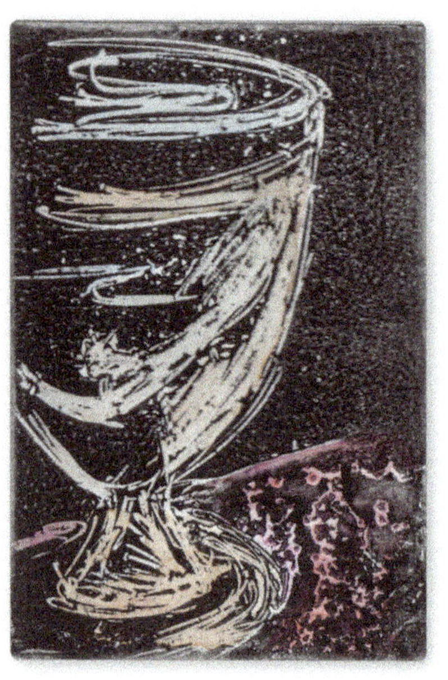

it is best to rise from life
as from a banquet,
neither thirsty nor drunken.

— Aristotle
philosopher & scientist
founder of western philosophy

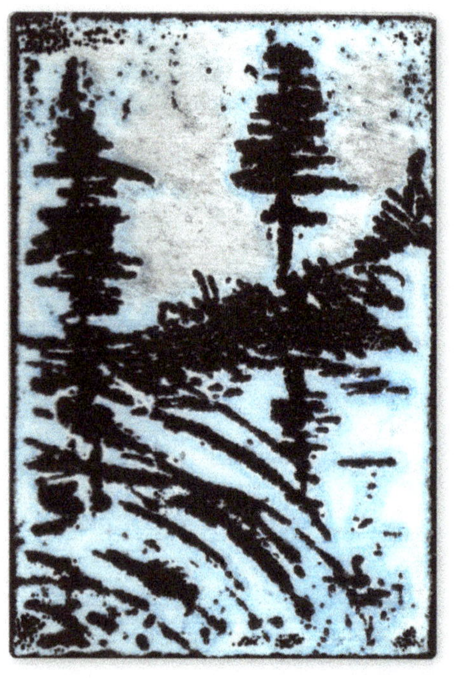

the real voyage of discovery consists not in seeking new landscapes, but in having new eyes.

— *Marcel Proust*
novelist, critic & essayist

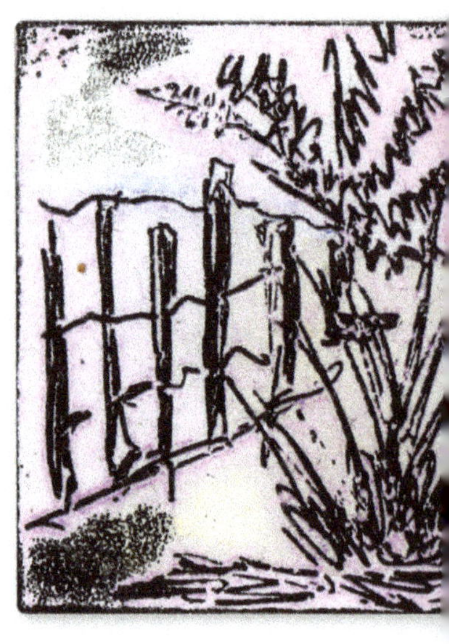

there is a condition worse
than blindness

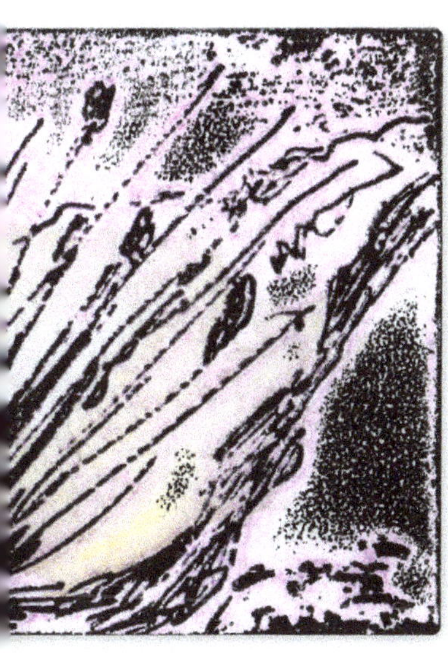

and that is seeing something
that isn't there.

— *Thomas Hardy*
novelist & poet

image titles

The *quotable impressions* series of small prints in this book are available for purchase. These limited edition prints are similar in size to those presented in this book. The title of each print corresponds to the originator of each quote and are numbered on the above list as Artist Version (AV≠) or Artist Proof (AP). Each print is an individual and unique work of art and comes with a Certificate of Authenticity. To purchase prints, contact dawndaisley@yahoo.com. To view these works and other printmaking techniques, visit www.DawnDaisley.weebly.com.

Dawn's early life was on South Shore of Long Island. At a young age she established water, boating, beach environs and natural habitats important to her development. She relocated to Manhattan and enrolled at Parsons School of Design in Graphic and Communication Arts in her early twenties to study graphic arts, believing it was the visual language of her generation.

Dawn feels that instant information retrieval through technology has a significant effect on current visual literacy and how it references our daily lives. She believes combining art, science and technology will be the future of artistic expression — art that speaks of a culture and its people.

Dawn continued her education at Pratt Institute and found purpose, confidence and self-awareness of her abilities as a learner, teacher, and artist. She felt enlightened by art history, philosophies and histories of education. When in graduate school completing her master's, she fell in love with printmaking and ceramics. Dawn is a resolute learner and seeks to extend her skills and sensibility through the medium of printmaking. She unites various experiences with different venues using new technology combined with traditional methods of art.